From Idea to Story
in 90 Seconds

Also by Ken Rand

Fiction
Bad News From Orbit
Dadgum Martians Invade the Lucky Nickel Saloon!
Fairy BrewHaHa at the Lucky Nickel Saloon
Golems of Laramie County
Phoenix
Soul Taster: Four Dark Tales
Tales of the Lucky Nickel Saloon
Through Wyoming Eyes

Nonfiction
The 10% Solution
Dan Colchico: In Defense of Port Chicago
The Editor Is IN
Human Visions: The *Talebones* Interviews
In Their Own Words: the Port Chicago Letters

From Idea to Story in 90 Seconds:
A Writer's Primer

Ken Rand

From Idea to Story in 90 Seconds
A Media Man! Production
May 2005
Copyright © 2005 by Ken Rand

All Rights Reserved

Media Man! Productions
1498 Bora Bora Drive
West Jordan, UT 84084
www.sfwa.org/members/Rand

Cover and Book Design by Patrick Swenson

ISBN#
1-933846-01-1

For Patrick, friend and mentor

Contents

Part One: THEORY
10 Ch 1: Where Do You Get Your Ideas?
17 Ch 2: One Question, Two Answers
20 Ch 3: The Cosmic Stew
23 Ch 4: The Antenna
33 Ch 5 : One Brain, Two Minds

Part Two: PRACTICE
48 Ch 6: Making *Media Man!*
53 Ch 7: The "Dare to be Bad" Challenge
56 Ch 8: Pilgrimmage
65 Ch 9: The Tinkerbell Zone
73 Ch 10: Write Quick, Not Good
82 Ch 11: We Dance
85 Ch 12: Advanced Idea Development
90 References

Part One: Theory

Chapter One:
"Where Do You Get Your Ideas?"

At any writers' conference, workshop, seminar, or similar event, somebody will ask a professional writer where he or she gets their ideas. It can happen any time: at a panel, a reading, a signing, or in a room party, a hallway, a restaurant, a bar, a restroom, on an elevator, in the question-and-answer session after the Guest of Honor speech, at the airport, or during an awards ceremony.

Professional writers expect it. Many dread it.

Their answers vary based on their personality, what they had for lunch, the numbers on their last royalty statement, how tight their underwear is, or the alignment of the stars.

The answers vary in content and style, but they are too often impatient, dismissive, callous, uncivil, contemptuous, unresponsive, or simply too short.

Harlan Ellison once wrote, tongue planted firmly in cheek, that he gets ideas from a service in Toledo. They send him a few ideas a month, he uses what he wants, and sends the rest back. In another article, he wrote that his idea service was in Schenectady. Roger Zelazny also said he subscribed to the Schenectady service.

To be fair, many pro writers do try to answer the question, or at least be civil to the asker, knowing they too faced a similar quandary when they started writing. They recall they too were once amateurs.

Pros know that often the asker just wants a magic bullet. The asker wants to be an *author*, rather than a *writer*. The difference between "author" and "writer" is akin to the difference between "refuse disposal technician" and "garbage collector." It's more than semantics — it's attitude: Authors *have written*, or, rather, *want to* have written. Writers *write*.

Still, seeing how easily a pro knocks off bestsellers for big bucks, how effortless her prose seems, how poised, confident, glamorous, and rich she appears, the asker thinks there must be some secret. "Tell me your secret," the asker pleads, "so I can be rich and famous, appear on Oprah, and have nice hair like you."

It's the amateurs' fundamental, naive assumptions that prompt many pros' discomfort with the question. Pros *know*. They've been there. What can they tell the novice who wants a shortcut? "There ain't any." "Write every day." "Success is ninety percent perspiration and ten percent inspiration." "Apply the seat of the pants to the seat of the chair." "*Scribendo disces scribere*": (By writing, one learns to write.)

All true, but also all stale answers to a stale question.

I spent more than two decades as a reporter (not a "journalist") and editor for newspapers and radio asking questions some people didn't want to answer. Hogwash and balderdash ruffled my feathers, and I prided myself on my doggedness (though not on my mixed metaphors). I've embarrassed politicians saying things like: "A fine speech, Congressman, but you didn't answer the question. Shall I repeat it?"

So, when I first heard the question (if I ever asked it myself, I've conveniently forgotten) I wondered what was going on. Why do pro writers respond to the question like politicians with dirty laundry or a cat with feathers in its teeth?

What was the *answer*, and why couldn't they spit it out?

The answer—*an* answer (lest we forget Kipling's nine and sixty ways)—came to me in my work as a reporter, and while writing a few thousand nonfiction articles and interviews, two-hundred humor columns, more than a hundred short stories, and two dozen books.

Ideas *do* come from a definable, understandable "somewhere," and finding ideas—*and translating them into story*—is not a mysterious process. Everybody taps the same idea source in much the same way. However new you are to writing, and no matter what you write—fiction or nonfiction, any genre, any length, and for any purpose, be it commercial, academic, or hobby—you can come up with more ideas than you can use in a lifetime. Anybody can get good story ideas any time, any place, in any circumstances—instantly. And do it over and over again.

You don't need to carry notebooks wherever you go to scribble every observation, every over-heard restaurant chat, idea, suggestion, or comment. You can if you want to, but you don't *need* to.

More, and straight to the point: anybody can come up with a Good Idea in *ninety seconds or less*. Equipment required: none. Not even a pencil.

This book will show you how.

For commercial writers—those who write for profit, whether fiction or nonfiction, freelance or staff—knowing where ideas come from and how to generate them fast may lead to more sales, to better markets, for more money.

For the student writer, understanding the process may lead to better grades.

Hobby writers may find greater satisfaction in expressing themselves better.

For all writers, knowing where ideas come from and how to get them will lead to greater productivity, greater reward, and a permanent end to writer's block.

First, I'll discuss where all artists, young or old, new or pro, no matter their artistic discipline, experience, or degree of talent, go to mine ideas. Theory.

Then, I'll demonstrate how I use this theoretical base to come up with story ideas instantly. Practice.

I tried to sell an earlier incarnation of this book as a "how-to." Several (too many!) publishers rejected it, citing two main reasons: it's too short, and it's too heavy on theory and too light on "how-to."

Yes, the book is short. It's no longer than it needs to be to get its idea across. A writer's time is best spent practicing his or her craft—writing—rather than reading "how-to" books, even this one. Besides, my background as an editor compels me to "eschew surplusage," as Mark Twain put it.

It took a while to realize, though, that the book is as much a "why-for" as a "how-to," if not more so. Why a "why-for?" As John Gardner put it: "Seize the trunk of any science securely, and you have control of its branches." E.D. Hirsch Jr. wrote: "Once the relevant knowledge has been acquired, the skill follows." And from James Webb Young: "In learning any art the important things to learn are, first, Principles; and second, Method. This is true in the art of producing ideas."

In the practice section, I do demonstrate how I do it, but I also emphasize that my method is modular; that is, writers will adapt it to their own way of doing things, and no one will—or *can*, for that matter, as I'll explain—do it exactly as I do. I believe that once a writer understands the theory behind the methods described — that is, how the brain functions in the creative process—they will naturally, *inevitably*, develop their own way of applying the theory. The practice section, then, is simply a demonstration of one way to do it—the theory at work. It's by no means the only way, or the right way. It's my way. That's all.

A "why-for," then, not a "how-to."

Still, you may opt to "cut to the chase," and skip the theory section for the nitty-gritty part. Go ahead. I believe, though, that you'll want to go back and read the theory section anyway before you get too far, if for no other reason than to satisfy your curiosity and confirm your own insight.

Or maybe not. While there are common patterns in the process, which I'll discuss, it seems to me that people do learn "differently," or at least at different rates, and people retain, or absorb, different specific elements of any given broad subject to varying degrees of depth. I'm not an educational psychologist, so I must respect the possibility that some learners will take a different tact to this material. I believe that any good book must respect that possibility.

Some people will take "why" and intuit "how" naturally. That's the way they seem to learn. Others want to go straight to "how," and figure out "why" later, if at all.

One premise I repeat often in these pages: "If it works, let it."

Learn as you see fit.

Theory and practice mirror each other in style and tone, but for purposes of organizing this material, and for emphasis, I present theory first, practice second.

I use the techniques described here to come up with short stories and novels and humor columns, but they might also be applied to create poems, scripts, and nonfiction articles. Writing nonfiction books is different, not merely as a matter of length, or degree and scope, but of technique. But even for longer, weightier projects, these techniques may prove useful.

Remember the old adage: "Give a man a fish and he'll eat today, but teach him how to fish and he'll eat every day." You'll learn how to develop your own ways to get ideas—methods tailored to your own skills, ambitions, vision, and life rhythms. Inevitably, you'll describe your own methods in your own vocabulary, not mine.

Actor and martial arts legend Bruce Lee posted on his school wall:

"The truth in combat is different for each individual...

1. Research your own experience.
2. Absorb what is useful.
3. Reject what is useless.
4. Add what is specifically your own."

This is good advice for writers as well as martial arts students.

Make no mistake about it — you'll find no magic bullet, no secret formula, no easy path to riches and fame here. As Aeschylus warns, "He who acts undertakes to suffer." Steven Pressfield in *The War of Art*: "[The professional] sustains himself with the knowledge that if he can just keep those huskies mushing, sooner or later the sled will pull in to Nome."

You *will* have to work hard to succeed as a writer, however you define success, and both luck and skill *will* play a part in whatever you achieve. You'll have to learn the skills and make your own luck.

But you'll never worry about coming up with a Good Idea ever again, and you'll never need to take more than ninety seconds to do so — ever again.

Chapter Two:
One Question, Two Answers

Pros answer "the question" with variations of two broad statements: "There are no new ideas," and "Ideas are a dime a dozen."

The two sound contradictory.

Both are true.

How can that be so?

There are no new ideas. No one has come up with a new story plot since before Gilgamesh. Georges Polti's *The Thirty-Six Dramatic Situations* covers the archetypal bases — or thirty-six of them. Robert Tobias enumerates *20 Master Plots.* Robert A. Heinlein counted three (Boy Meets Girl, The Little Tailor, One Who Learns Better). Historian Will Durant said, "Nothing is new except arrangement." Voltaire said that originality is nothing but judicious imitation.

Ideas are a dime a dozen. When Harlan Ellison does signings or similar events, he'll often sit in a bookstore window at a desk with his typewriter. He'll open a sealed envelope somebody has given him. In it will be "an idea." The challenge: write a story — finished, ready to publish — based on "the idea." Do it without stopping, and finish it — *today.*

People watch through the store window as Ellison raps away. Each page goes from typewriter to window, taped there for people to read as it's being written. No editing.

Chapter Three:
The Cosmic Stew

The world is covered with an invisible fog, floating two feet above our heads. It has no odor and no taste. You can't touch it or weigh it or measure it. It never goes away.

Most people don't even know it exists. Artists know. When discussed, it goes by many names. When defined at all, it is too often poorly defined.

I call this fog the *Cosmic Stew*. Carl Jung called it the cosmic unconscious. To help you grasp the concept, you may invoke psychologists, philosophers, theologians, Itzhak Bentov, Joseph Campbell, Carl Jung, Marshall McLuhan, Zen Buddhist masters, mystics, or others who have theorized, analyzed, pontificated, or rhapsodized about the subject. Much has been written about a mass human consciousness, unconsciousness, or subconsciousness — the Cosmic Stew. Some thinkers use the concept to explain dreams or headaches or schizophrenia or clairvoyance or mass murderers' psychology or why people bite their fingernails or vote for the other candidate.

I'm a writer, not a scientist or philosopher. Whether there is a measurable, quantifiable "place" or phenomenon called the cosmic unconscious, or subconscious, or the Cosmic Stew, or whatever, doesn't matter, really. The concept as I'm using it here is a metaphor that helps me understand where ideas come from and how to translate them (perhaps *transcribe* is a better word) into story. This book is a user's manual, and while it emphasizes theory, it is nonetheless not a doctoral dissertation. I don't gotta show you no stinking footnotes.

If the notions presented here are more Lewis Carroll than Carl Jung, let it be. If it helps turn ideas into stories, it works. The Cosmic Stew, as a concept, works for me.

In this stew are those thirty-six plots Polti talked about, Tobias' twenty, and Heinlein's three. What artists "judiciously imitate" are the images and ideas in this stew. Here are the archetypal symbols Jung wrote about. Freud poked around in the Cosmic Stew to find out why little boys hate their fathers. Here is where you'll find Joseph Campbell's universal myths. Here is where Don Juan led Carlos Castaneda. Here is where Timothy Leary tuned in, turned on, and dropped out. This is the Spirit World, Nirvana, the Force. Here is where the shamans go, and the eastern mystics, the gurus, and the yogis. This is where we all go to dream, daydream, have nightmares, hallucinate, get visions, and ideas. This "large reservoir of information produced by all mankind," as Itzhak Bentov calls it in *Stalking the Wild Pendulum*, is where every artist, every writer, gets ideas. "What if?" lives here. "Eureka!" lives here. Stephen King, Norman Mailer, Mark Twain, William Shakespeare — and *you* — every writer who ever wrote, or who will ever write, drinks from the same cup.

This has been true from the time millions of years ago when the first true human told the first story to the first audience. Storytelling is the first human art.

The Cosmic Stew, this universal storehouse of all consciousness, is where story ideas — where *all* ideas — come from.

When someone asks, "Where do you get your ideas?" they're trying to de-mystify this fog, to define it, describe it. To gain access to it. Pros have figured out how to tap the Cosmic Stew *in a controlled, routine manner*, and instantly. Amateurs have not — yet.

Learning how to control the flow of ideas from the Cosmic Stew, and translating them into *original* stories, is what this book is about.

Now, how do we tap into the Cosmic Stew, and turn those images into original stories?

Chapter Four:
The Antenna

Bentov asserts that "our brain is not the *source* of thought, but a *thought amplifier*," and that "thought does not originate within the brain; rather, the brain picks up the tiny impulses implanted there by our astral, mental, or causal bodies." In other words, our brain picks up and amplifies signals from The Cosmic Stew. How?

You have an antenna. This is what you use to tap into the Cosmic Stew. You stick your antenna up into the Cosmic Stew as it floats above your head and the antenna relays, like a radio receiver, images from the Cosmic Stew into your brain.

All people tap the Cosmic Stew through dreams. Our antenna taps into the stew, draws into our brain images — sounds, story lines, vignettes, dialogue bits, seemingly random fragments of patterns, plots, scenes, events, emotions, incidents — *dreams*. Nightmares, daydreams, visions, hallucinations, and all artistic and creative notions, insight and inspiration stem from the same universal source — the Cosmic Stew — and are tapped by the same instrument, the antenna.

All people tap into the Cosmic Stew unconsciously. We have no choice but to sleep and to dream. Writers and other creators tap the Cosmic Stew consciously, deliberately, and routinely. We try to control the process, not only while asleep, but when we daydream, or think about story.

Your antenna is your personal access to story ideas. It's important to understand how your antenna works, how to use it, tune it — *focus it* — to access the Cosmic Stew well and at will.

Your antenna is part of your brain.

No two brains are alike, as no two people are. That's because environment is the key ingredient in shaping our antenna into a controllable, Cosmic Stew-tapping, story-grabbing instrument.

Here's the good news — you can shape your environment at will.

No two people are alike, or as Jung put it, "the shoe that fits one person pinches another." While it sounds obvious, it's relevant in understanding where ideas come from and how we translate them into story.

No two of us will ever tell the same story.

Irving Wallace once heard a professor tell a student "Everything has been written about already, and written better than you can do it." His response: "Everything has not been said, and will never be said. Human emotions may have always been the same [i.e., there are no new ideas]. Still, there was never anyone on earth before you who was exactly like you and who saw love and hate exactly as you see them through your eyes."

Consider too that an estimated one quadrillion nerve connections exist within the brain, so that at any one time, the possible combination of messages jumping across the synapses *exceeds the number of atoms in the known universe*. What this means is that the potential reservoir of stories in your head is, practically, infinite.

You and I may — *will* — tap the same archetypal image. But because we grew up in different neighborhoods, see the world through different cultural heritages, have different social concepts, religious beliefs, educational backgrounds, family relationships, and because we speak a different language — or different dialects and jargon in the same language — that is, because *we have different memories* — we'll never tell the same story no matter how detailed the "idea" on which the story we're both telling is based. We can't, because our antennae are different, our memories are different, and we transcribe the signals from the Cosmic Stew in language particular to those differing memories.

A writer's group conspires to write short stories based on a common idea, plot, or theme. "Let's each write a romance about a two-headed cowboy astronaut who loses his pants in a poker game in the X dimension." As many different original stories emerge from any such contest as there are participants. Theme fiction anthology editors exploit this concept for profit.

Darrell Schweitzer has joked for years that *Alternate Historical Vampire Cat Detectives* is only a matter of time. He wrote a story for it. "The Adventure of the Hanoverian Vampires" appeared in the anthology *Crafty Little Cat Crimes* (Barnes & Nobel, 2000).

(An important corollary: "A word is not a crystal, transparent and unchanged," Oliver Wendell Holmes said. "It is the skin of a living thought, and may vary greatly in color and content according to the circumstances and the time in which it is used."

Moreover, no two readers will — or can — ever "get" the same thing from the same story, no matter the circumstances. Carl Jung wrote in *Man and His Symbols*: "Each word means something slightly different to each person, even to those who share the same cultural background. The reason for this variation is that a general notion is received into an individual context and is therefore understood and applied in a slightly individual way. And the difference of meaning is naturally greatest when people have widely different social, political, religious or psychological experiences."

John Gardner agrees: "There are limits to the extent to which people of one culture can imaginatively embrace the experience of people from another."

For example, if I say, "pony," what mental image do you get? Circus pony? Indian pony? Or something else entirely? No writer will ever achieve one hundred percent clarity in conveying their thoughts and images, as Holmes, Jung, and Gardner point out. Hence, mastering the language — *practice* — is a major component of all writers' efforts. Professional writers know this, while they also understand that, no matter how hard they try, no matter how much they practice, no matter how well they master their craft, they'll never get closer than, say, ninety-nine percent to their reader. More: they'll never *know* how close they get. This doesn't stop them from trying, day after day.)

To return to the point, we can change our environment at will — or perhaps better stated, we can change our *relationship* with our environment at will. We make such adjustments routinely, daily, sometimes minute-by-minute. Any athlete will tell you that we even change our environment second by second. We do so when we change our *physiology*, our *brain chemistry*. "The most important thing about visual images," Ronald Shone writes in *Creative Visualization: How to Use Imagery and Imagination for Self-Improvement*, "is that they can influence the body." Since our brain is this Cosmic Stew-tapping antenna, when you change antenna chemistry, you change the antenna's tapping capability.

Carlos Castaneda would recognize this concept. Timothy Leary's LSD-induced hallucinations are duplicated all over the world in various cultures. Shamans, visionaries, mystics, and spiritual guides in all cultures throughout the world, "primitive" and modern, alter their brain chemistry to open the spirit world door and peek in, or walk around inside it. They inhale fumes and eat from selected, processed plants with specific chemical characteristics, take sweat baths, fast, suffer sleep and sensory deprivation, and physical tortures. They dance, sing, chant, drum, hum, whistle, and rattle—make carefully controlled rhythmic noises—vibrations—and motions, all designed to alter brain chemistry—to access images within the Otherworld.

Bentov writes: "our brains produce rhythmic electric currents," and "The body as a whole will be affected by gravitational or magnetic effects." In *Remembering*, F. C. Bartlett wrote that memory is active and constructive rather than passive and reconstructive. I contend that our relationship with the Cosmic Stew is not just active—it is *interactive*. That is, we take from it universal images as the foundation of our creativity, and using our individual memories as the material from which we construct our own stories, we give back to the Cosmic Stew new — original — stories from which future generations may draw.

We all connect with the Cosmic Stew. For better or worse.

What did you eat for lunch? Got a sniffle? Back ache? Stress at work? Financial problems keep you up nights? Trying to quit smoking? The answers to such questions related to your physical well-being are also answers to how well your antenna taps the Cosmic Stew. If life is tossing you constant 95-mile-per-hour beaners, you're too busy ducking to write worth diddly.

If you eat right, exercise, play well with others, enjoy life — love yourself, and all that hippie New Age stuff — you'll write better. Shone invokes meditation when he emphasizes that best creative visualization results "when the mind and body are in a relaxed state." You'll write better because your antenna will be tuned better. It won't be coated with life's interfering gunk — and life sends us too much creativity-inhibiting gunk. When you stick it into the Cosmic Stew to tune into ideas, ready to suck them down and translate them in your own individual — *original* — interpretation, you'll get a better signal if you first tune your antenna.

Clean up your act. Relax. You are what you eat, literally (*literarily*) and figuratively — and you write what you are.

I don't suggest you take illegal drugs to get cool hallucinations. Various drug-using writers' occasional literary brilliance is a side issue. Let's not go there. The side effects, including the legal hassles (not to mention the jail food), aren't worth it. There are easier and cheaper ways to tune your antenna.

Since no two antennae are alike, no two ways to tune antennae will be alike.

The best drug ever prescribed, in my opinion, is *placebo*. (Until recently. I've switched to New, Improved Instant Placebo®, in mint-flavored gel caps.)

The "placebo effect" works. If you believe sharpening all your pencils before you write will help you write better, then it will. If you believe having a grinning, green ceramic frog next to your computer will help you write better, it will. If you believe that you write better after drinking two low-fat mocha grandes, brown sugar, no cream, thank you, then you will. If you believe you get better ideas in the morning rather than at night, then you will. And so on. We *create* environment, willfully, and live (or die) within the environment we create.

If you *believe*, you *will*. "A *mighty will*," Henry James said. "That's all there is!"

Will is the key ingredient in priming your antenna — in altering your brain's chemical characteristics — to tap the Cosmic Stew better.

Or not. You will yourself toward achieving whatever you want to achieve, consciously or unconsciously, for good or ill.

Unfortunately, some of us will ourselves toward self-destructiveness rather than self-discovery and self-realization. We say to ourselves that sharpening pencils and playing endless games of solitaire help us prepare for the Muse when what we're really doing is lollygagging, lying to ourselves, giving in to our fears and delaying getting on with the task at hand. Will can be both truth and falsehood.

Fortunately, we can tell ourselves truth, and we can control what lies we tell ourselves. We can, and should, tell ourselves *good* lies, because such lies can, and will, become true—this is what the placebo effect does. I have a friend whose e-mail address is, in part, "darngoodwriter." Darn smart, too.

It's easier to control antenna aspects closest to the surface—in terms of time, that means closer to now—than aspects more deeply and firmly embedded in our neural net. It's easy to change your mind about what to do in the next hour. It's less easy to change dinner plans for this weekend, but still doable. It's hard to get a divorce or get married. It's harder to think about changing nationality. It's harder still to consider changing one's religion. Few people think about changing sexes, and it is impossible to change races so nobody thinks about it.

Editors recognize this hierarchy. Marketing is based on recognizing that, beginning from the broadest base—"We are all human"—divisions emerge with decreasing numbers per subdivision.

Thus, genre fiction exists. Publishers know broad readership characteristics overlap—and groups shape-shift. It drives publishers crazy. Their marketing department people get paid to try to predict genre subdivision populations and changes.

Everyone has personal rigidity that we cannot transcend. The deeper these aspects of our psyche are buried—the more hardwired they are—the less we are able to change them, or to even recognize they exist. The less flexible we are—the less flexible our antenna is—the less adept we'll be at sucking creative juice from the Cosmic Stew. Rigidity, dogmatism, incuriosity, laziness—such attributes don't belong in the writer's toolbox. Eric Hoffer's True Believer is more likely to be a pedagogue, or a propagandist, than a True Artist. Yet all humans possess these ill-suited attributes (ill-suited to the creative mind-set) to varying degrees.

This "hardwiring" of our personal worldview is more than metaphor—it is a well-studied, quantifiable, scientific, physiological concept. The term "hardwiring" effectively describes what happens in our brain when we learn.

Listen to what Dr. Carla Hannaford write in *Smart Moves: Why Learning Is Not All In Your Head*: "Neural plasticity is an intrinsic, beneficial characteristic of the nervous system which gives us both the ability to learn, and the ability to adapt in response to damage—to relearn. From shortly after conception and throughout a lifetime, the nervous system is a dynamically changing, self-organizing system. It follows no single master plan and is never static. We develop our neural wiring in direct response to our life experiences. Ability and increased potential grow hand in hand. As we grow, as we move, as we learn, the cells of our nervous systems connect in highly complex patterns of neural pathways. These patterns are organized and reorganized throughout life, allowing us greater ability to receive outside stimuli and perform the myriad jobs of a human life."

In *Mother Tongue: How Humans Create Language*, Joel Davis writes: "From the moment of our birth, each of us lives through a unique set of experiences, and our brains process each and every one of them. Each sensory experience, each person we see, each sound we hear, each pain or pleasure we feel, the brain processes and stores. As it does so, it builds up its network of interconnected cells and neuron clusters."

Davis adds, echoing Jung: "Our brains are very plastic during our infancy and early childhood. There is plenty of room for improvising on the basic structure, as it were. As it responds to its particular set of experiences, each brain creates a network that is slightly different in structure and connections from every other."

Repetition of experience is physiologically related to learning, adapting. You never unlearn how to ride a bicycle. Repeato: "Donde esta el bibliotheca?" "You're stupid and you'll never amount to anything." "I'm proud of you." "I hate you." "I love you."

Write the next story. Do it again. Again. Get into the habit of *doing*. The habit of *doing* can and will transcend the usually more powerful habit of *not doing* — if you *will* it so.

New ideas thrive on the borderlands, the frontier. While brilliant prose has been written intending to reinforce the community, little *original* material — art — has emerged from such intent. This is what Joseph Campbell means when he says you have to go outside the community to get new material. The community has a vested interest in the status quo — the community *is* the status quo. "Don't color outside the lines."

So tune in — and write on.

Chapter Five:
One Brain, Two Minds

When I wrote *The 10% Solution: Self-editing for the Modern Writer* for Fairwood Press in 1998, I'd been using the methods discussed in the book for almost thirty years, writing as a reporter for newspapers and radio and as a PR "flack" and as a freelancer and in other capacities, to try to make my prose more accurate, clear, and brief. I hadn't thought much about where I got my editing technique. I just did it. One day, while writing *The 10% Solution*, I stumbled onto a book about the editing theory I'd been practicing.

I knew what I was doing, instinctively. *Writing the Natural Way*, by Gabriele Lusser Rico, articulated and quantified the theoretical basis for my practical, self-taught knowledge.

Rico writes about left-brain right-brain theory and its relationship to creativity. She says that "there are at least two distinctly different aspects of any creative act that sometimes come into conflict: the productive, generative, or 'unconscious' phase; and the highly conscious, critical phase, which edits, refines, and revises what has been produced." The right brain is the creator; the left brain is the editor.

Our brain hemispheres have different functions, but generally, they work and play well together. Most people can walk and chew gum at the same time. We don't notice.

As a baby matures, brain functions become more coordinated, more integrated—and more rigid. We are born right-brain dominant, internally focused. Experience, interaction with the external physical world, the world we perceive through our senses, produces left-brain dominance.

Now, combine the left-brain, right-brain concept with the Cosmic Stew and the antenna notion. It's easy to imagine the antenna is not just your brain—but your *right* brain.

Here's how it works:

You're in that fuzzy area between sleep and wakefulness when you get an idea for a story. It's vivid in your mind. The characters are alive, the dialog sings, the plot compels. It's got all the Good Stuff. You think you've got it—The Greatest Story Ever Written.

You dash to your computer, being careful not to trip over the cat, turn it on, and write. Your fingers fly.

A few paragraphs or a few pages into the story, you stop—you *quit*—and check your e-mail. You toss The Greatest Story Ever Written into a drawer, virtual or real, with all the other Greatest Stories Ever Written, as your alarm rings and you get dressed for your day job.

What happened?

While dreaming, your antenna extends into the Cosmic Stew, grabbing random images—neurons are firing, making seemingly random connections. You're like a dog in a car passenger seat with its nose out the window, smelling the scents in the wind as you go down the road.

Most signals you perceive are weak and indistinct. You touch them, sniff, and move on. They're not the droid you're looking for. In fact, because they're so inconsequential, you don't remember them. It is as though they don't exist.

Our left brain does the same in the physical world. Our senses are active all the time when we're awake, but our left brain filters out the signals we don't need and can't use, and lets in only the Good Stuff. This prevents sensory overload, so we can keep our eye on the ball.

This is how it happens with most of us. We seldom remember dreams when we wake up, and when we do, it's in faint bits and pieces. Even the most vivid dreams appear as shadows when we play them back in our memories seconds after we awaken.

Now and then, one idea stands out, vivid in the misty dreamscape, and lingers.

You lock onto one scent—your antenna tunes in to one idea. (I told you I'm metaphor challenged.) It stands out in the Stew, a large, succulent lump of meat among bland veggies and broth, and you gobble it up.

Your antenna downloads this idea for you to realize as a dream because before you went to bed, consciously or not, you tuned your antenna to find it. Maybe you were worrying about your job or sex life when you dozed off, priming your antenna to find images related to those thoughts. Maybe, like many writers, you went to sleep thinking—*deliberately*—about a particular problem, a plot complication you wanted to solve, or a character flaw you needed to fix. You went to sleep thinking about *this* problem— priming your antenna—and you have *this* dream.

Listen to Ray Bradbury talking about how he wrote *Fahrenheit 451*: "I made a conscious effort to think about the novel before I went to sleep so that my subconscious would give me answers when I woke up. Then, when I was lying on bed in the morning, I would say: 'what was it that I was working on yesterday in the novel? What is the emotional problem today?' I wait for myself to get into an emotional state, not an intellectual state, then jump up and write it." In other words, he *consciously* sublimates the left-brain editor ("the intellectual state") and empowers his *unconscious*, his right-brain creator ("an emotional state").

Consciously, then, as Bradbury and other writers do, or unconsciously, as we all do, we "program" our dreams. We tune our antenna before we enter sleep, or similar relaxed states, right-brain dominant, just as we tune a radio. Want news? Dial up *this* station. Want rock music? Dial up *that* one. When you focus on one signal, your brain filters out the others and you don't hear them.

The more vivid the dream, the more likely you are to remember it as you wake up. Many times such dreams will feel like The Greatest Story Ever Written when you wake up.

But right after you wake up, your left brain starts to dominate, to organize the world around you. Your left brain puts you in the center of the universe. You relate to the physical world from the center outward. The five senses begin to relay messages to your brain. This is a Good Thing, because it keeps you from walking into walls or tripping over the cat on your way to your computer.

But it's a Bad Thing, too, because your left brain has no patience with unrealistic right-brain namby-pamby artsy-smartsy hippy-dippy mumbo-jumbo. Too chaotic. To your left brain, the ideas in your head are noise to be filtered out. They distract the left brain from keeping you upright, from helping you shave without cutting off your ear. Your left brain functions well enough without Art, thank you very much.

If the right brain is noise to the left brain's important work of helping us get along in the physical world, the left brain is noise to the signals the right brain receives from the Cosmic Stew. Faced with the Very Important and Very Busy left brain's noisy bullying, the wimpy right brain shuts up, goes into its cosmic corner and pouts. The left brain wins because when we are awake we live in a left-brain-dominated—a physical—world.

Try this experiment. The next time you drive up to a stop light, one that you know takes a long time to change, if there is at least one car ahead waiting for the light to turn green, don't pull all the way up to the car and stop three feet behind as you normally do. Stop two car-lengths behind. Then wait until the car behind you stops. It'll stop three feet behind you, as everybody does. Now, give the person in the car behind you a couple seconds to relax and look around. Then, pull ahead—three feet. Watch as the car behind you pulls ahead three feet to fill the six-foot gap you just left. Now, wait a few seconds, until the driver behind you starts looking around again, bored. Then, pull ahead three feet. The driver behind you will fill the six-foot gap, close it to three feet. You can repeat this trick three times, but no more—or until the light changes. Then, it doesn't count anymore. Three times. By then, the driver behind catches on and stops playing.

Why does this happen? The six-foot gap you created when you moved up is disorder in the universe, as the left brain of the driver behind you sees it, be-cause "as everybody knows," there's "always" three feet between cars at stop lights and in traffic jams. The driver's left brain orders the driver to fill the gap. Filled, his left brain can go on idle again and he'll start looking at billboards. Create the gap again and his left brain gets agitated again.

Ever notice birds on a telephone wire? Exact spacing.

Wait, there's more: how awkward did *you* feel stopping your car two car-lengths behind the car at the stoplight? Most people feel odd leaving such a gap.

Here's another one. At any gathering in a room where a number of people who don't know each other are converging, like a seminar or workshop, arrive early, stand in the back of the room, and watch how people decide where to sit. They will divide the room into equal parts, sitting as far from one an-other as possible. The second person in the room will divide the room in half, the third arriver will try to divide the room into thirds, and so on. This is done automatically, unconsciously. As the room gets fuller and fuller, you'll see people becoming more and more uncomfortable as they see they must sit next to somebody.

Don't believe this phenomenon is real yet? Try this: after only three or four people have arrived in the room, sit right next to somebody, in the next chair, elbow-to-elbow. Be friendly about it. Watch how uncomfortable, even belligerent, your victim gets. And notice how uncomfortable others in the room get even when they're not the victim of your little experiment.

Dare not try this? Ask yourself why not.

Another experiment, a variation of the last one, to bludgeon the point, then we'll move on.

When you're at a meeting or workshop or conference or similar function among total or relative strangers, maybe in a hotel conference room where many chairs sit in rows or around tables, wait until after the speaker declares a break. Before the break is over, sit in a different chair. Don't sit in a chair "claimed" by a coat draped over it, and stuff on the table in front of the chair. Pick one that looks as if it may not have been occupied, but you know it was. Make sure there are many empty chairs in the room or this experiment doesn't work as well. Now, sit. Then, when the former occupant returns — the person who sat there before the break — watch her actions. She may say something like: "Hey, that was my chair." If not, she will look and act uncomfortable, annoyed, or even angry.

"*Your* chair? It belongs to the hotel. *That* chair," you point to the one you occupied before the break, "is empty. Why don't you sit there?"

How uncomfortable did you feel even *considering* this experiment? Sweaty palms? Why? Your left brain tells you where your center is, and when you sat in that other chair, you grew uncomfortable because it wasn't your center.

Don't try these experiments at an Anger Management Seminar. Come to think of it, the car-space game could provoke road rage. Space violation, as illustrated by these three "games," is so important that people get killed over it.

A school of fish. A flock of birds. People.

Having centered the universe around us, we are now ready to manipulate it, to control it.

Have you ever watched people bowling? They'll twist and gyrate after they've released the ball down the alleyway as if their movements, in violation of the laws of physics, might have some magical influence on where the ball connects with the pins. You see, not only do we perceive the world around us, or rather, do we perceive ourselves at the center of the universe, but we have the gall to believe that we can rearrange the universe with mind power alone to suit our particular desires or whims.

On a broader scale, that people believe the spiritual world has an impact on—indeed is more important than—the physical, is reinforced in every culture; it's too often the underlying meaning and purpose of most wars: "My God can lick your God."

Our left brain creates order in the physical world around us—*from the center outward*—and where we are *right now* is the center of the universe, as far as our left brain is concerned. It doesn't take long for a strange chair in a strange room to become "our" chair in "our" room—and the center of our world. In seconds, our left brain adapts to an environment, and *organizes* it. When we move, we reorganize, quickly, again.

Since we're the center of the whole universe, why *wouldn't* our attempts to change the physics of a bowling ball not work?

These experiments illustrate the personal-centering concept of group and personal spatial relationships, but it also shows how we relate to the world in a broader sense. We perceive reality from the center (our left brain) outward, and our writing, and other expressions, reflects this *centeredness*. We can't help it. This is why no two people will ever write the same story.

So, the left brain dominates our waking state.

The right brain will be back, later in the day, when the left brain gets bored. You'll give your left brain a rest from writing a report or planning a presentation with a game of solitaire, for example, or you'll doze off during that mid-afternoon meeting, "just resting my eyes." In other words, you enter a relaxed state, and your right brain will sneak up front and announce the answer to a problem that has baffled you for a week. Or you'll be doing the laundry or the dishes when your right brain will come up with an elegant way out of that plot hole you dug yourself into the day before.

Writers Lois McMaster Bujold and Connie Willis say washing dishes is a good way to get ideas. Showers are good too. Something about warm, soapy water lubricates the right brain—or perhaps "liberates" is the better word. In some desert, mountain village, or tropical jungle, dishwashing is part of a shaman's ritual access to the spirit world, and lemony fresh liquid detergent is an important ritual talisman. Lawn mowing works for me.

The right brain will always be there, and it'll speak up, when the left brain takes a break. You won't always be near your computer, tape recorder, or notepad when it does. And as soon as it does, the left brain will begin to beat it into submission again.

Why is your left brain such a jerk?

Because writing is a mechanical, linear, sequential, left-brain activity. It is a physical act, and the physical world is the left brain's realm. When we write, we organize meaningful, remembered sounds and sights — sensory images — into symbols, that is, the rigidly organized alphabet.

Your left brain hates disorder. So, when your right brain starts writing a story, your left brain, if not leashed, will interfere, even before you finish the first word, phrase, or sentence.

"What's this junk?" your left brain nags your right brain as you write. "Call that a paragraph? Who taught y'all grammar? Hey, incomplete sentence! Your point of view character is an idiot." And so on.

Left-brain noise drowns out your right-brain signal as you translate the signal image into symbols to represent your story.

The interference is immediate. An unfinished story is disorder. An unfinished sentence is disorder, so your left brain is on the job before you know it, literally. The left brain hates disorder, so it hates incompleteness. It will hound your right brain to get in line, sit up straight, and chew each bite thirty times.

Finishing a story would give order, but to stop writing and throw it away — *now* — also satisfies the left-brain mandate for orderliness. Quitting is easier, faster, and less painful. The left brain is more satisfied with immediate, easy answers. It has a lot of Important Work To Do so it filters input fast, categorizing, discarding irrelevant impulses, and organizing what it keeps.

So at the first sign of left brain resistance you toss the story aside. It *was* a wonderful idea, a good plot, and it might have been a good story if you'd finished. But, like so many writers, and most people, you give in to your left-brain bully.

Thus, writer's block.

Now, some writers will occasionally muscle their way through the resistance, but too often, such brute force efforts result in what John Gardner calls "aesthetic arthritis," which is "the disease that ends up in pedantic rigidity and the atrophy of intuition." Better writers recognize when this is happening even as they're doing it. They call it "hack work." Readers often can tell the difference, even if they don't know why.

Writer's block, or pedantic rigidity.

Don't berate yourself. Every writer's left brain tells him or her to Give Up.

The trick is to muzzle the bully, to *focus*, to concentrate. Concentration, Ernest Dimnet writes in *The Art of Thinking*, "is the elimination, one after the other, or by sweeping effort, of all images foreign to a train of thought."

But how can this be done with the left-brain bully watching over our shoulder all the time?

"People dominated by one great passion," Dimnet writes, "apostles of all degrees, live in their mastering purpose and do not need exterior solitude to think." Writers write on busses, on subways, in crowded restaurants and theaters, all left-brain dominated atmospheres. For all creative apostles, the external noise is sublimated to an internal voice that demands greater attention. Thus, the absent-minded professor. Thus, the seemingly serendipitous revelation during states of relaxation—that is, when the right brain is ascendant and the left brain subdued. "Eureka!"

All successful writers, you see, have split personalities, metaphorically speaking. They can activate the right-brain creator—*at will* (even if it seems to have occurred serendipitously) while shutting up the left-brain critic, shutting out the outside noise and focusing on the inner signal. Later, they reverse gears, muzzling the right brain while the left brain edits and markets.

Some writers do this with cybernetic implants, but they're hideously expensive.

This is how most do it:

Sit your hemispheres down and negotiate what I call the Hemisphere Accords. Your left brain agrees to shut up while the right brain downloads ideas from the Cosmic Stew, develops those ideas, and writes the stories that result. In turn, your right brain agrees to not whine when the left brain takes over and edits, then markets the results.

You might need trickery to get your hemispheres to cooperate. For example, in *The 10% Solution*, I suggest you wear a hat labeled "writer" when you write, and one labeled "editor" when you edit. Write upstairs, edit downstairs. Write in the morning, edit in the afternoon. Write naked, edit dressed. Whatever. These things signal to your brain: "I'm wearing my writer hat, I'm upstairs, it's morning, and I'm naked. Must be time to write." Brain-training routines. Creative visualization. It's the placebo effect in action. It's lies—but *good* ones.

When we alter our brain chemistry, deliberately as writers and other creators do, or serendipitously as everybody does, miraculous things happen. Solutions come to us in elegant and complete detail and form, as if we knew them already but are at the moment *just remembering*. This is exactly the case. The answers are all there in the Cosmic Stew. All you're doing to remembering, or as Itzhak Bentov writes, "the solution was received when the mind momentarily happened to be in an altered state of consciousness."

Relax. Let it come.

Your brain-fooling techniques will be different from mine (different antennae, different chemistry). Experiment. Find out what works, and go with what works for you. After a while, you might not even notice the little rituals you perform to will yourself into different brain hemisphere-dominant modes. You may even believe you don't engage in such self-control, that you don't alter your brain chemistry through such silly techniques. You'll just do it. And it'll work, because you *will*. Because you *believe* it will.

Successful writers and other artists use this technique, as they always have and always will. They describe it differently, if at all, but it's the same idea.

For instance, the guy who wrote "The Battle Hymnal to the Republicans" is said to have dreamed it all, word for word. Archimedes took a nap in a bathtub where he discovered hydrostatistics. Alexander Graham Telephone dreamed the solution to a problem that led to the invention of the telephone solicitor.

Shamans and vision questers do it all the time.

Michelangelo, Leonardo da Vinci, Shakespeare, Socrates, and Einstein dreamed. All tapped the Cosmic Stew with minimal noise, maximum signal.

You can do it too.

Relax. Let it come.

To summarize, and to re-connect with our original scenario, when someone asks: "Where do you get your ideas?" they mean, "How do I get my left brain to shut up while my right-brain antenna taps the Cosmic Stew to best effect? How do *you* do it?" Your answer: through the Hemisphere Accords and the "placebo effect," you deliberately subdue the left brain while the right brain does its work, then switch gears.

Next: How I do it.

Part Two:
Practice

Chapter Six:
Making *Media Man!*

From 1988 to 1991, I edited a small rural weekly newspaper in Delta, Utah. The *Millard County Chronicle Progress* had a circulation of about 2,000. I gathered news and took pictures for the front page, and filled the editorial page with editorials, cartoons, and letters. I wrote a humor column, *Media Man!*, for the editorial page.

On Friday afternoons, I left the office. Every other weekend, I drove to Salt Lake City to visit my kids and ex-wife. On alternate weekends, I drove out to the desert. I brought a tape recorder on those trips, desert or city.

I set out to think about next week's *Media Man!* column, and record ideas for it. I set out with my antenna primed thus: The column would be humorous, 750 words long, and about a specific topic. The topic would be something in the news, like an election, the weather, my cat, war in Iraq, or the city council's decision to build a new toilet for the city park.

Armed with tape recorder, and a primed antenna, I drove.

I took the back road, never the freeway. Why? The object wasn't just to get there. Arriving ten or fifteen minutes later (than what?) didn't matter. The object was *going*, and tapping the Cosmic Stew on the way. The freeway is more left-brain intensive than the back road—fewer idiots try to kill me on the back road.

I drove the back road to sublimate left-brain interference in the Cosmic Stew-tapping ritual, and activate my antenna as much as possible.

I didn't speed or listen to the radio. I drove alone. Relaxed.

I recorded ideas, dialogue bits, questions and answers, jokes, quirky juxtapositions, funny lines, "Aha's!", Andy Rooneyish "Didja evers?", titles, structures, lists, narrative flows, and anything that might belong in next week's column. I tried to suck the Cosmic Stew for all the gravy I could get in the ninety-minute or so trip. The left brain would interfere now and then to keep me from driving off the road or hitting a cow, but I was *focused* so I'd return to my right-brain activity after my left brain handled whatever crisis happened to cross the road ahead of me. I arrived at my kids' house with thirty to forty-five minutes of *Media Man!* material to digest.

Then I'd set the tape recorder aside and not think about the column until Sunday afternoon when I got home.

When I got home, the first thing I did after feeding the cat was write as much as I could remember from two days earlier, paying no heed to spelling, grammar, order, punctuation—all that left-brain folderol—as I did so. I became a right-brainish, fast-typing fool.

It didn't take long before I'd exhausted all I could remember from Friday afternoon. I'd usually type 800 to a thousand words or more in one sitting of twenty to forty minutes or so. Remember, I'm aim-ing for a 750-word column.

Monday, I'd open the *Media Man!* file, edit, add things I'd forgotten, and tinker with phrasing, order, grammar, spelling, structure and so on. The same Tuesday. Ditto Wednesday.

Thursday, I listened to the tape. I'd find a cool joke I'd forgotten, or a better title than the one I'd used all week, or I'd switch this line *here* with that one *there*. And so on.

I found, though, that I remembered almost ev-erything I'd taped, and I made few changes.

Why didn't I just listen to the recorder Sunday night? Why wait until *after* I'd written the column, relying just on memory, to listen to the material I'd taped for the column?

Relying just on memory. That's why.

When I was in my Cosmic Stew-tapping, driv-ing-on-the-back-road mode, I set down on tape—aloud, to reinforce the memory—the biggest Stew chunks, the pieces that floated to the top easiest, that cruised down the deeper neural pathways in my memory bank. If these pieces came with so little thought or effort, I figured it would be the same for any reader thinking about the same subject. So, when I wrote this line, or that joke, it would likely strike a familiar cord with most readers.

That's what I looked for in the column. I fo-cused—tuned my antenna—on the most interesting thing happening that week. Then I looked for the most direct images from the Cosmic Stew associated with the news—the bigger chunks, the ones I got with minimal effort—because more people would recog-nize those images.

That's why I relied on memory. The taping ritual reinforced memory. After my Sunday night, right-brain word-dumping binge, writing the column was mostly left-brain editing and organizing.

Thursday night or Friday morning, I did the *10% Solution* editing ritual (a left-brainer), turned in the column, and started on next week's. Lather, rinse, and repeat.

Did it work? No subscriber ever shot at me. And I never missed a deadline. Never. Not with *Media Man!* or anything before or since.

Still more: I did this every week at the *Chronicle-Progress*, then for a newspaper in Wyoming, then after I started freelancing "semi-fulltime." I sold every column. I've sold columns to the *Seattle Times, Buffalo News, Monterey Herald, Gauntlet,* and three dozen other magazines and newspapers.

Several columns have appeared in print a dozen times, and I've earned good money from those columns over the years. I came up with more than two hundred columns, all written the same way, using the same ritual to alter my antenna chemistry to better access the Cosmic Stew.

To summarize the key elements in writing *Media Man!*:

1) I set out determined to accomplish a specific task. Having a deadline helped enforce this will.
2) I primed my antenna Just So. I ordered my right brain to seek out images in the Cosmic Stew related to the task at hand.
3) I established left-brain-sublimating, right-brain-activating rituals. The back road trip. No radio, no speeding, minimum worries.

4) The ritual included tape-recording the images downloaded from the Cosmic Stew. This helped me remember those images, so I'd later summon their most common elements.

5) I followed with a specific routine to translate those images into a column, edit it, and turn it in on time.

There's no secret in what I did with my humor column in five years of combined salaried and freelance writing. Pros with regular deadlines, whether they write fiction or nonfiction, establish rituals in a similar manner. Some writers who aren't already under such pressure impose arbitrary deadlines on themselves (although they may call them "goals," it's the same thing) because they understand such internal pressure helps make them more productive. Writer's group "challenges" accomplish the same thing. Left and right brain interaction is, for most of us, unconscious. For successful writers, separation of brain hemisphere functions is deliberate and natural.

As it will for you, after you've done it a while.

Chapter Seven:
The "Dare to be Bad" Challenge

In 1992, I re-married my ex-wife, ending a nineteen-year divorce (the divorce wasn't working), and began a "semi-fulltime" career as a freelance writer. I wrote fantasy and science fiction short stories, indulging a life-long passion for the genre.

By 1995, I still hadn't made any significant fiction sales, what anybody might call "a pro sale." I studied craft, tried to figure out what needed doing, and how to do it. I practiced.

I took part in the now-defunct GEnie science fiction roundtable discussions on-line. That's where I heard about the "dare to be bad" challenge. The "dare to be bad" challenge is a mainstay in writer's groups and on-line communities. The concept is designed to help stuck writers get unstuck through a kind of group therapy, a "we're-all-in-this-together" support thing. The "novel-in-a-week" challenge familiar to romance writers is the same concept.

The GEnie SF roundtable challenge was to write three stories in six days.

I decided to try. I knew I could do it since I'd written a few stories, most in a week or so each.

I finished the first two with no problems. I suspect I already had story ideas for those two before I started the challenge, but I don't remember. I had no idea where to start the third.

I asked for advice from the GEnie group on how to find an idea for the third story. One person advised thus: Go to a supermarket and observe someone at one end of the store. That's your protagonist. Go to the other end of the store and note another person: your antagonist. Put the two together and let them interact. There's your story.

I thanked my advisor (whose name I've unfortunately forgotten) and went shopping. By the baby formula, toilet paper, and cat food, I saw a tired, frumpy, fortyish woman pushing a half-empty cart. In produce, I found her twin. Same bored look, same stuff in the half-full cart, same frumpy, fortyish demeanor. Tweedle-dum and Tweedle-ditto.

Disappointed that I hadn't gotten two interesting opposites to face off in a story, I left via the ice cream aisle. There, I passed a couple looking into the freezer. He weighed ninety pounds and stood five feet tall. She was twice his size. She held an ice cream brick and berated him in what sounded like Italian. I didn't understand a word until he grabbed the brick, put it back, and took out a different brand. Gesturing wildly, he said the ice cream he held had "no calories."

Epiphany!

I left the store, my head buzzing. By the time I got home, I had a story. I lived a half mile away.

I wrote three stories in six days. In 1997, one story, "The Gods Perspire," appeared in *L. Ron Hubbard Presents Writers of the Future*, volume thirteen, a second-place winner in the contest. I earned $1,750 for that story, and an expenses-paid trip to Florida where I watched a Space Shuttle launch and attended a productive, intensive professional writers' workshop with other winning writers.

The other two stories sold later.

Not bad for a week's work.

What happened in the ice cream aisle? How did that encounter turn disappointment at not getting story material from the two shoppers into a story idea by the time I got home, a five-minute drive? How did the Italian couple help make story idea jump from the Cosmic Stew into my head as if my antenna were a lightning rod? (Now, *there*'s a useful metaphor.)

Why did *three* elements suddenly jolt my brain into story realization where *two* did not?

Those first two shoppers didn't provide enough imagination stimuli to draw a coherent signal from the Cosmic Stew. They weren't specific enough. They were two balanced elements, tending toward equilibrium, toward zero signal, canceling each other out. I was frustrated, but I didn't know why until I saw the Italian ice cream couple. Then I intuited that my antenna needed *three* elements, not two, to be primed to draw idea from the Cosmic Stew. The realization hit so fast, and came so fully formed, that I had a story by the time I got home.

What happened, in practical terms, was that the Italian ice cream couple epiphany gave me an idea expressed as a simple sentence, a *subject, verb, and object* (three elements), which I then used as a catalyst to create a story. I later formalized this process while writing a story a week.

Chapter Eight:
Pilgrimage

This is how I did it:

In 1996, I was in a writer's group called Pilgrimage. The other members lived in Provo or Orem. I live in Salt Lake City, a forty-five to fifty minute drive north. I drove down Saturday evenings for the meetings where we critiqued our manuscripts and then went out to dinner.

At dinner, I'd take the first noun Bruce Franklin Thatcher used in conversation as my *subject*, the first verb Scott Bronson used as my *verb*, and the first noun Lee Allred used as my *object*. Next week, I'd reverse the speaker's order, or listen to other members. Random selection. Didn't matter.

Armed with a subject, verb, and object, I made a sentence. For example (This is taken from David Farland's *Brotherhood of the Wolf* because the book is within arms reach at this moment): "horse" (subject), "begs" (verb), "clothes" (object). These three words, randomly picked from three different pages of text, become the sentence: "The horse begs for clothes."

Now, with the S-V-O (subject, verb, and object) sentence, selected at dinner, my antenna was primed with these imperatives: 1) short story, 2) science fiction or fantasy, 3) humor, and 4) the SVO. Thus primed, I drove home.

Back road, of course. Alone, no radio, no hurry. The process resembled my *Media Man!* idea development phase except I didn't use a tape recorder. I talked to myself, sometimes aloud, most often not.

Why no tape recorder? For *Media Man!*, I sought the common elements — clichés, if you insist — because I was writing humor, and an essential ingredient in successful humor is *identification* with readers. In *The Craft of Comedy Writing*, Sol Saks writes: "Close to identification are the qualities of the familiar and recognizable, comfortable and friendly elements that can make laughter so much more readily forthcoming." But for my short stories, I wanted more than common archetypal images, expressions, patterns, tropes, and notions. I wanted greater *originality*.

At this point, I must relate to you what Orson Scott Card said several years ago at the SF-fantasy symposium *Life, the Universe, and Everything*, held in Provo each year. Card said the first idea a writer comes up with is a cliché. Don't write a story based on your first idea. It's been done.

Have you ever written a story where the pets were Adam and Eve, "and the planet we abandoned them on was — *Earth*!" Have you ever ended a story with "And it was all a dream?" Have you ever started a story with your main character *waking up*? Did you ever have your character *look in the mirror* and describe herself?

Clichés.

A cliché story is based on the largest chunks in the Cosmic Stew, the images and ideas most people share, commonality at the cultural level. Joseph Campbell and Carl Jung fans will recognize this concept.

Card suggests you give your first idea a 180-degree turn. Still, you're just getting started. Many writers, as clever as you but not more, will follow the same "what if" path down which you turned, so you must go one better. The third turn may become a good story if you're as good as the best writers, but for most of us, it's wiser to take the fourth turn. I take the fifth — and beyond. There, Card contends, is where you'll find originality.

In terms of my metaphor, this means you must keep your antenna in the Cosmic Stew longer, search past the bigger idea chunks, the "group-think," and savor the rarer, more exotic elements that are more distinctly your own. If you just get your antenna tip wet, you ain't got game. Keep fishing.

You're engaging in "the process of masticating these materials, as you would food for digestion," according to James Webb Young. "What you do," he writes, "is take the different bits of material which you have gathered and feel them all over, as it were, with the tentacles of the mind."

When I say "keep you antenna in the Cosmic Stew longer," I don't mean that the answer, your "Eureka!" moment, will take a long time to arrive. It may, or it may not. Revelation may come to you at three a.m., when it jars you to sudden wakefulness. It may arrive hours or even days after you've mentally started the process of querying your subconscious mind for the answer. What I mean is that when the answer comes, it's common that it does so *instantly*. It is as if all the unconscious mental mastication of the problem you want to solve has come to some kind of critical mass, and your subconscious delivers in fully cooked and ready to serve. That "mastication" takes place unconsciously, so you're unaware of the clicking synapses making patterns. Only when the pattern is complete, only when it gets delivered into your conscious mind, do you become aware of it — and then, you're aware only of the result, not of the process that went into getting there.

Consider: some pro magazine editors read 800 short stories *a month*. A story you think is original is one they've seen a zillion times. You took an idea refined to pea-sized fineness and submitted a story based on it. Good, but the editor uses a finer sieve to discern originality — pinhead size.

A related phenomenon: One editor gets a dozen stories the same month about a baby's goo-gooing summoning demons. Another gets a batch of stories where the hero is named Henri and the love interest is named Alexandria. Who knows why, but this happens. Jung used the word *synchronicity* to describe such phenomena.

Another way of looking at what's happening with this process is that by digging deeper into your Self you'll reach your passion — *your* passion — or at least get closer to it, and so be able to bring it to the surface of your consciousness where you can transcribe it into story.

By "passion," I don't necessarily mean that you should seek in your mind's core what you *like* or *admire* or *appreciate*. As Annie Dillard wrote: "A writer looking for subjects inquires not after what he loves best, but after what he alone loves at all."

Eschew the "safe." C.J. Cherryh advises: "Be as hard on yourself as you can be without destroying your spontaneity. Don't be afraid to attempt a book, an idea, even if you don't think you can do it." Louisa

Swann says: "Write what you fear. Write from your heart. Write the stuff that makes you cringe, makes you want to change your name, move to a new country."

Remember how each antenna is different, yet we each have much in common? Your first antenna twist in the Cosmic Stew taps just the broader, general elements. When you twist your antenna a second time, penetrating deeper, so to speak, you've tapped the Stew with greater individuality, yet common elements remain, the tenacious influence of the stronger elements of our cultural heritage. So, you're still in a realm shared by other writers — brothers and sisters of the same subdivisions. The third twist centers your antenna closer to who you truly are, so you see the ideas in the Cosmic Stew through more individual eyes. At the fourth and later twists, you're examining the finer stuff in the Stew, doing so with an exclusive, individual eye no other writer can duplicate. You're centered. You've reached originality, your passionate inner Self.

Knowing this, after getting the S-V-O antenna primer at dinner with my Pilgrimage comrades, I tried to turn my antenna as many times as possible in the forty-five-minute to hour-long trip home. Why did the horse beg for clothes? How? What kind of horse, and what kind of clothes?

I'd take the S-V-O and try first *this* "what if," then I'd add *that* complication, revise the first "what if" based on the new twist, discover an "Aha!", then see if a new "what if" emerged that I'd then apply to a different setting, new or different character or characters, or a new problem layered over the premise, or I'd see if the evolving plot might be better expressed as a sword and sorcery fantasy rather than a dystopian near-future SF yarn, or alien planet setting, or I'd tilt away from humor toward a serious tone, or I'd decide maybe I should consider it in first person rather than third, at which point I might decide my original idea for the point of view character ought to be *this*, not *that*, and I'd find another "Eureka!," which in turn provided the insight to consider changing or reversing protagonist and antagonist, which in turn might lead me to conclude I was on the scent of a Really Good Idea — *and I haven't left the parking lot yet!* — which always alerts me to try another "what if" because I forgot how many times I've turned my antenna in the Cosmic Stew so far, and I still have forty-five miles to go and maybe I should consider theme, which I usually consider later, and if that will help me find another "what if" layer which might in turn help me find more complexity or more narrative nuance, or another character attribute that may help add another layer to the story, deepen the intensity, or the humor, or the general story appeal. And so on. Allllll the way home.

Try it. Take a kitchen timer and set it for ninety seconds. Take a book near at hand. Don't *choose* one. Choosing is left-brainy. Just grab. Open it at random to page X, read until you see a noun. Write it down. Then flip through X pages and read for the first verb you see. Again don't *choose*, just grab. Write it down. Ditto for another noun.

Make a sentence with the three words, a subject, verb, and object: your S-V-O primer.

My predisposed genre preference is science fiction and fantasy, but this method works for any genre

(I'm using the term in its broadest sense here: let's not get into "my genre is better than yours, neener, neener, neener," please). As readers, we are all predisposed to appreciate certain genres over others. Your writing will naturally reflect your reading tastes, and you may have other antenna primers pre-established, such as humor, or female point of view, or other such factors. Predisposition—antenna pre-tuning—may seem inhibiting, but it's not. All ideas, all genres, have boundaries. Stories get written within those boundaries. Marketplace alone doesn't create them. They exist within a story, and within a writer. It's a Good Thing for writers to know where boundaries are of their stories, and of themselves. (Then *push* them!)

Mystery readers expect a murder to happen, and for the detective to name the killer by the end of the book. Romance readers expect the girl to get the guy. Science fiction readers know what FTL means and are off-put if you try to explain it. Sword and sorcery fantasy readers drink yeasty mugs of ale, not Bud Lite.

Recall the problem I had finding a primer in the supermarket before the ice cream aisle epiphany. Two elements weren't enough to prime my antenna. Three worked.

Knowing other pre-tuned elements beforehand, like genre, point of view preferences, and so on, at least in general form, and what sort of a story you want to write, *based on whatever idea you find in the Cosmic Stew*, can help you find the good ideas faster.

With your S-V-O sentence written down, start your timer. See how many twists you can give that silly sentence, how close you can come to having a coherent story ready to write based on it. If you feel you're on to something, don't stop. Twist the elements you think are working as solid story ground. This will lead to other changes, which will in turn—well, you get the idea. Let the ideas flow. Do it aloud. Go fast—*fast*. Try it.

(At this point, I'm going to discourage you from trying this with a partner. Sometimes two heads are better than one, but not here, not now. Here, now, you want to develop, to exercise, your own creative imagination. You're trying to see what's in your own head, hear your own inner voice. You don't want that voice edited by another's, not now. I'll talk about the efficacy of brainstorming, of "group-think" or "sound-boarding," later.)

What you'll get from this exercise, if you take enough time (idea twists as Card might say, or probing into the Cosmic Stew with your antenna longer and deeper, I'd say), is an original story that may have little or no resemblance to the original idea. That's okay. In fact, if you stick to the original sentence too closely, you're allowing your left brain to interfere. Your left brain will try to make you stick to your original sentence, because to do so is *orderly*. Separate the brains. Let the right brain *go for it*. Originality is what you're after.

Although I've done this exercise hundreds of times, I remember only one idea that became a story. The rest are dust in the wind. The idea that I remember: Butch Cassidy and Sundance Kid, with the bank loot, run from the posse. The two bandits hide in a cave, where, as the posse closes in, they find a time machine and escape. A novel emerged from this scene. And yet, the only element *Pax Dakota* has that resembles the original idea is *the cave*. That's it.

After almost an hour twisting one nonsense sentence around, you'd think I'd be ready to write. No, I have two final steps, antenna twists, before I convert my mental image through word-symbols into a story.

Chapter Nine:
The Tinkerbell Zone

Step second-to-last:
I'd take a story I'd culled from the Cosmic Stew to bed, looking for yet another antenna twist. I dreamed.

Recall that earlier I discussed will, the placebo effect, how you can take your problems with you into dreamland, and dream, or have nightmares, about them. Or you can prime your antenna with a story line concocted through self-talk and many antenna twists of your S-V-O primer. That's what I took to bed. I tried to dream about the story.

It is said that you can program your dreams. The process is called "creative visualization," "lucid dreaming," and similar terms. While some books make the concepts seem a bit far out and New Ageish — more commercial than scientific — many writers and researchers approach the subject seriously (Shone comes to mind) and the results are generally useful and instructive. I'll go where the lessons are to be had. I'm after metaphor, remember, not science or pseudo-science. While this book recognizes and discusses theory, it is still, in the end, a user's manual, not a doctoral dissertation.

Anyway, I try to stay on track as I go to sleep. My left brain shuts down as I first close off sight, then the other senses. The right brain takes over and leads me into dreamland.

Later, I remember—

—nothing, it seems. I believe the process works, that taking an S-V-O primer into the Cosmic Stew helps turn idea into story. *Does* it work? I don't remember.

"What? You present a scheme to turn ideas into stories and you recommend a step you don't know even works?"

Believing something works is different from knowing something works. Faith is right-brain— knowledge is left-brain. The mechanics of human consciousness is a slippery subject. The mechanics of creativity may be a sub-category of consciousness. Even scientists and other smart people don't agree on how the mind works. (Some pundits, like Bentov, even dispute whether "mind" is located in the brain!)

But let me take a stab at it (remember, I'm interested in metaphor, not in science).

First, I'm trying to separate my left brain and right brain so my right brain can tinker with idea and story more efficiently, unimpeded by the left-brain bully. The left brain is a 500-pound gorilla when I'm awake. Why let it intrude on my dreams, which is right-brain territory? My brain hemispheres, remember, made an agreement in the Hemisphere Accords.

Second, remember the placebo effect. The first ingredient in the placebo effect is Will. I believe all the silly rituals that I go through to come up with ideas work, ditto my writing and editing rituals. It seems natural to believe taking a story to bed is an effective step in converting idea to story. I *will* it so.

Third, I can't prove it *doesn't* work.

Will. Placebo effect. Deliberate separation of left and right brain authority.

So, I'll take a story to bed, and dream about it. Eight hours or so later, in the realm between sleeping and waking, which writer-editor-publisher Rebecca Shelley calls "The Tinkerbell Zone" (*Hypnagogic*: from awake to asleep. *Hypnapomic*: from asleep to awake.), I'll creatively visualize, or lucidly dream, another story element, or an alteration or variation or elaboration or clarification of an existing one.

Hurry to the keyboard before the image is lost.

Oops. Too late. A page or two into the story and I will have likely forgotten the dream.

But it doesn't matter. It seems the images conjured during sleep, and during the foggy stage before and after sleep, are retained *unconsciously*. I can't tap them consciously (left brain) but they are there, ready to be tapped (by the right brain) *when and as they're needed*. Left brain is intellectual, right brain is emotional, as Ray Bradbury tells us.

"Unconscious" seems to be the right word here, but "retained" may be misleading. That's because memory is involved. Joel Davis writes (in *Mother Tongue*): "If the process of creating memories were purely linear, grounded in physical brain structures, book reviewers would not have Harold Robbins to kick around and Tom Robbins to praise. Creating new worlds, characters, events, and jokes out of thin air requires a different process, one in which the brain can recombine fragments of memories in a myriad different patterns that are not immutably tied to 'reality.'"

This is why I try to take the road less traveled, not the well-worn path, try to drive the side street, not the freeway, why I always try to leave and arrive early, so I'm not in a hurry and can stop and smell the roses. I have eclectic reading habits (and I read A Lot), meet new people, eat new foods, go different places and get there by different routes, and embrace new experiences as often as I can.

What I'm doing is filling my memory with material to draw on later when I'm writing. Or as James Webb Young puts it: "The more of the elements of that world which are stored away in that pattern-making machine, the mind, the more the chances are increased for the production of new and striking combinations, or ideas."

My memory pantry is well stocked with the ingredients to take me through the scenes I want to write, and to do it effectively, with fresh, vivid imagery. (I hope. Mastery of craft, translating the images I draw from my memory pantry to effectively communicate those images to a reader through the symbols of the alphabet, is an important and never-ending aspect of the creative effort, a detailed discussion of which is outside the scope of this book.)

Of course the learning process is never over. Writers continue to learn new things, constantly, throughout their careers. Insatiable curiosity is a common trait among writers and other creators, and one that can easily be cultivated. The fact that school is never out is one of the most fun and intriguing aspects of this job.

Writers should never drive on the freeway. There's nothing new there. Sign up for the group tour, but ditch the guide at the first junction. Eat calamari—at least once. Read a romance novel—it's good for what ails you!

But I don't keep a notebook or journal, as many writers do, to jot down this snippet of conversation overheard in the restaurant or that plot idea I got while mowing the lawn or details about some weird character I saw in the mall (although I keep paper and pen handy for business notes: addresses and the like). Many writers believe they need to jot these things down so they won't forget them, to better recall them later.

I don't do so because I know that, *exactly when I need it*, the appropriate memory will surface for me to use. The tapped memory *will* be distorted, because its recall is triggered in response to the action demanded on the page. As the scene unfolds under my fingertips, I tap my memory for the sensual images — sounds, sights, tastes, smells, textures — appropriate to that scene, *and that scene only*. The memory — retrieved without conscious (left-brain) effort — is *molded*, if you will, to fit the needs of the scene unfolding (right-brainishly) on the page. And it comes exactly when needed.

Or look at it this way: What if, every time I run across a particular activity, or bit of dialogue, or new character, or similar element in a scene, I flip through my carefully indexed and dated and catalogued notebooks and journals (in other words, go to the left brain) to find the exact referent that I'd written down six months or six years ago? What would the reference tell me, if I can in fact find it? "You are reading this note because the project under your fingertips *right now* has prompted you to recall this image. Since you already remember it, why do you need to read this? The action is redundant, dummy. It's all there in your right brain already. Go write!"

Memory, as Davis notes, is a slippery subject, as consciousness and creativity are. Memory is fluid and not subject to ready scientific scrutiny and easy categorization and analysis.

But never mind all the scientific mumbo-jumbo. Just remember that your memory is your source, instantly tapable, for all the information you need to accomplish any task you might have in front of you. No — you don't even have to remember *that*. Just go write.

Here's another metaphor, another way of phrasing the above: Memory is a buffer, like RAM, between the Cosmic Stew (right-brain dominant) and the waking state (left-brain dominant). Just tap the mental key labeled "go fetch," and the proper file opens.

Now, there *are* writers who swear by the efficacy of writing down serendipitous observations in notebooks and journals, and some writers who do so use the experience to great effect, bless them. Teachers say that we retain a greater percentage of what we hear or see if we write it down. Writer-friend Julia West consults her journals when she finds herself in a plot bind. Somewhere in her notes, she believes, is the answer to get her out of trouble and get the story moving again. For her, the journals aid her right brain in getting back on track.

Bravo. Remember my initial caveat: if it works, let it.

Warning: Many writers use journalizing and notebooking to expend their creative energy, an unconscious way to avoid actual writing (that is, the left-brain bully's sneaky way of getting the right brain to twiddle its thumbs). My advice: Trust your right brain to do what needs doing when it needs to be done. Trust your inner Muse, and don't diffuse or misdirect her energy by taking notes excessively.

So, then. You wake up, having tried to program your dreams, and having dreamed, and then — forget the dream as you sit down to write? Is it possible to remember a dream without remembering that you remember?

Maybe. Something is going on, I *believe*, even if I don't *know* what it is. Call it magic. Jung writes in *The Undiscovered Self* that "magic has above all a psychological effect whose importance should not be underestimated." As long as whatever's going on doesn't cause baldness (too late) or heartburn, I'll try it. Thus, I believe that a) I can take a story to bed, b) dream about it, and c) wake up with maybe unconscious, maybe unremembered, but still significant input into that story. I don't sweat it. When the time comes, I'll remember what to do next.

Will. The Hemisphere Accords. The placebo effect. Whatever works, let it work.

Finally, here's how James Webb Young summarizes the idea production process: "First, the gathering of raw material — both the materials of your immediate problem and the materials which come from a constant enrichment of your store of general knowledge.

"Second, the working over of these materials in your mind.

"Third, the incubating stage, where you let something besides the conscious mind do the work of synthesis.

"Fourth, the actual birth of the Idea — the 'Eureka! I have it!' stage.

"And fifth, the final shaping and development of the idea to practical usefulness."

What Young means by that last element is that after you get an idea, *you must write it down*. This is both harder and easier than you think.

Chapter Ten:
Write Quick, Not Good

Step the last:

Since my reporter days, I've become accustomed to writing fast. Oft heard in newsrooms from editors: "I don't want it *good*. I want it *now*." Deadlines are discipline. Deadlines help stimulate the right brain, sublimate the left brain. That's the purpose behind those timed exercises in creative writing classes. If you don't have a real and specific deadline imposed on any given project, long or short term, invent one.

So, I wasn't surprised to hear at a workshop in January, 1996, that writing a thousand words a day is doable and a Good Thing. Writing a thousand words a day relates directly to my concept of self-imposed deadline development.

Husband and wife writer-editor-publisher team Kristine Kathryn Rusch and Dean Wesley Smith have conducted a workshop designed to help newbies intent on making fiction writing a career. In what has come to be called "The Kris and Dean Show," they try to answer questions they wish they'd had answered for them when they were new writers.

One thing on which they insist: Write a story a week, and within two years you will publish at least one story in a professional magazine or anthology. A thousand words a day will get you a story a week.

Does it work? Starting in January, 1996, I tried to write a story a week. That year I wrote thirty-five stories, part of a novel, and a half dozen articles. In July, 1996, I made my first pro short story sale.

I've always written fast. I did so as a radio ad peddler (not an "account executive"), as a reporter, and after my "semi-fulltime" writing career started in earnest in October, 1992. I wrote those three dare-to-be-bad challenge stories, including that supermarket story, in six days.

I was surprised, then, to hear some writers gasp, indignant, at the idea, saying: "Fast writing is sloppy writing."

If writing fast makes sloppy, hackneyed story, then does writing slowly make *better* story?

If writing slowly makes a story better, consider this: If you take one week to write a story, would it have been a better story if you had instead taken two weeks? Twice as good if you take a month? How about six months? A year? Ten years? Follow this illogic and you'll find the story that *never* gets written, ever, is the Best Story Ever. *That's* the story that writers who huff at writers who write fast write (or *don't* write, rather).

The myth that to write fast is to write sloppy reveals a writer who has difficulty isolating the right-brain creator from the left-brain editor while he or she tries to write. Slow writers are blocked writers. Their left and right brains are at war with each other. What such writers *know* is non-productivity. Why would this be a useful thing to know, and what benefit is there in passing on such "wisdom" to another writer? Don't listen to people who *can't*, and who insist you can't either.

On the other hand, writers who have exercised appropriate brain chemical-altering rituals, taken their new and improved, minty-fresh, extra-strength Placebo® gelcaps, willed themselves into the proper mindset, and let their right brain do its job in its time, will realize story quickly and efficiently. They'll write faster because their left brain has shut up, waiting, as agreed in the Brain Hemisphere Accords, for its turn to edit and market. Such a writer will also write *more* stories, thus having *practiced* more, thus having *learned* more about the craft and how to communicate through craft *better*.

More ideas, more original ones, more efficiently received by the right brain, more effectively transcribed into story. More story. More money. More fun.

This is not new. Rico's *Writing the Natural Way* is one of a hundred books (one of the better ones) that explore ways to stimulate creativity through systematic and controlled brain hemisphere separation and isolation. Timed writing exercises are one well-known way to do it.

You may have heard a writer say: "The story wrote itself." This comes from one whose right brain is active and in control during the writing phase — the translation phase — of turning idea into story. Writers are unconscious of right-brain dominance *while it happens*.

Of course, each writer's life is different. Some writers lead intricate, busy lives juggling family, job(s), community, church, health issues, and other commitments while also trying to write. How some do it is amazing and awe-inspiring.

The prepared writer, the efficient writer, the dedicated, willful writer, *makes* time to write. She does so *economically*. She indulges in no solitaire or mind-drain games or similar left-brain lollygagging when it's the right brain's turn in the barrel. She writes fast now, edits carefully later.

Even if she has fifteen minutes to write each morning waiting for the bus, or a half-hour while the baby naps, a writer can be productive, if she wills her focus in that time to the task. Will is ingredient number one in the placebo effect needed to tune the antenna.

You know how slowly you can write—zero words an hour/day/week—but do you know how fast you can write? Try this exercise. Take a kitchen timer and set it for a half-hour. Write. Don't worry about spelling, punctuation, grammar, story line, coherency, or anything else. Just write. (Helpful Hint: turn off your spell and grammar checker when you're writing. Turn them back on when you edit.)

You've done timed writing exercises before, but a half-hour? It can be grueling. You'll find yourself (your left brain) watching the clock after five, ten, fifteen minutes. You'll be tired and sore. (Beware of repetitive stress syndrome!)

Or maybe not. You may surprise yourself and discover mental (and physical) strength and agility you never suspected.

At least you'll get a good fix on your top speed.

If you don't want to try the exercise, do the math. If you type at, say, thirty words a minute, you type 300 words in ten minutes, which is more than one typewritten page. Thus, you should be able to type three or four pages in a half-hour. Four typewritten pages (figuring double-spaced text in Courier twelve-point, with one-inch margins all around) average about a thousand words. To type four pages in one hour, you must average only about sixteeen-point-six words a minute. (By the way, that's my usual writing speed — and people call *me* fast!)

Write as fast as you can (right-brain active) now. Edit at leisure (left-brain active) later.

So, you *really* don't have time to write a thousand words a day. You're really *that* busy. Many people are — too many. Even if you aim at 500 words a day, or 250 words, or just one sentence, and you Do It Regularly, you're ahead of writers who lament they don't have time to write a thousand words a day and then write *none*. Some is better than none. Do what you can. Find out what you can do, then do it.

Don't overdo it. You'll be an unhappy writer if you miss your bus, or burn the roast. You'll be an unhappy writer if you set your goals unrealistically high, and then berate yourself for not meeting them. Both hurt your creative capability.

Don't *under*do it either.

What's your capacity? What do you want? Find out. Then go for it.

Finally, if you don't believe me about the utility and efficacy of writing fast, take this: "The faster I write, the better my output. If I'm going slow I'm in trouble. It means I'm pushing the words instead of being pulled by them." Raymond Chandler said that.

Now, what does this have to do with *step the last* in the idea-to-story process? Every successful writer has found, after a thousand, or 2,000, or 3,000 words or more into a short story — and for novelists, it can happen after 10-, 20-, 30,000 words or more — that what they just wrote *isn't the story after all*. After all the thinking, outlining, Cosmic Stew-tapping, antenna-twisting exercises they've gone through, they find the story they want to tell starts *here*, not back *there*. They find they must throw away thousands of words that *aren't* the story, that were just warm-up, just a matter of sneaking up on the story's real beginning.

In fact, it's standard pro writers' attitude to start a story conscious of a missing ingredient. Writer James Van Pelt calls the process "confident ignorance," which is "a faith that answers will come, and that it's all right that they aren't all there when the first word is written." Writer John Brown calls this "farmer's faith—faith that crap will bloom."

F. C. Bartlett writes in *Remembering*: "An individual does not normally take a situation detail by detail and meticulously build up the whole. In all ordinary instances, he has an overmastering tendency simply to get a general impression of the whole; and on the basis of this, he constructs the probable detail. Very little of his construction is literally observed. But it is the sort of construction which serves to justify his general impression."

(This has several implications depending on perspective. To the writer trying to come up with a story idea, this means every detail need not be in place to get started, as Brown and Van Pelt say. What it means in terms of craft is that only specific and relevant detail is needed on the page; the reader will take it from there, and it's up to the writer to determine what the relevant details are, and what constitutes too much or too little detail. What it means to the reader is that the clearer and more specific the details on the page, the better the reader will be able to "see" what the writer meant.)

Starting without knowing the end is most common, while not knowing how to get there is second most common. Some writers even start *without a beginning*. Pros know that missing elements will appear, eventually, as they write. But the elements can't appear *if they don't start writing*.

A slow, blocked writer may have difficulty tossing out a thousand well-honed words, but the fast writer knows the map is not the territory, the manuscript is not the story, and will have no such difficulty.

Consider the writer with only one story in the mail. This writer will wait at the mailbox for that story to come back, fretting miserably. One rejection could be seen as a statement about *a hundred percent* of the writer's inventory. Consider the writer with a hundred stories out. One rejection comments on only one percent of the writer's inventory. The reason why writer number two doesn't haunt the mailbox is that she's too busy writing her next story.

Which writer do you think will cope with rejection better?

And the writer with a hundred stories in her inventory will find it easier to cut thousands of words from a story if the words don't belong. This is one reason writing pundits say that your first million words are practice. It may be hard to see now, when you have a half-dozen stories on your shelf, but wait until you have a hundred. Then you'll know.

If I hadn't written a thousand words a day, religiously (I use the term fully aware of its meaning in this context), I could not have made the cuts I made. Writing a lot will help you better recognize where a story really starts, while it will also help you, brain-chemistry altered Just So, to Do It.

Why does it happen?

You start with an S-V-O to tune your antenna, then you twist it in the Cosmic Stew several times, then you sleep on it, and then you start writing. After all that preparation, you think you've *got the story*, and all you're doing now, Raymond Chandlerishly, is typing it as fast as you can. But something else is also happening. Your mind is still studying the story. Your right brain is still empowered to twist the story even more.

Your brain is never idle. Recall times when you'll be reading a book and your mind will drift, and you'll think about something other than the words on the page (and ask yourself why the writer let your mind wander). When we're bored, we daydream and doodle. Recall when you tried to twist your S-V-O and you found some buzzing fly, or cow in the road, or errant thought from your left brain, distracting you.

Your brain is never idle. If you don't put what you want into it—Will, the placebo effect, tuning your right-brain antenna—your left brain will jump in and you'll find yourself thinking about your taxes or your sciatica. Or your right brain will take over when the left brain goes on cruise control and you'll daydream.

Your brain is never idle. You can't turn it off.

If you've empowered your right brain to work—*now*—on creative story aspects, it will continue to do so into and throughout the writing phase. Writing is arranging symbols to represent story, which represents idea, so it's a left-brain activity, but it's done with the right brain *in control*, as per the Hemisphere Accords. In other words, as you write, the right brain, in control, is still active, still in contact with the Cosmic Stew. It still brings idea into story as you render story into symbol. Thus, you often discover that your first thousand or 2,000 words are warm up, the final antenna twist. The thing is still tuned in, and receiving signal.

This is also why pros will start a story without every story detail in place, using "confident ignorance," or "farmer's faith." Whether it's a missing beginning, middle, or end, they know they'll Get It.

This explains why you are capable — right now — of going from idea to story in ninety seconds.

Or less — I use "ninety seconds" as a convenience, and to create a clever title. I attended a workshop recently where we were assigned to turn a newspaper article into a short story. I read my assigned article as I walked the few steps — only two dozen or so — to my room. Fortunately my computer was already on because I had the story in my mind before I finished reading the first paragraph. I couldn't type fast enough to keep up with the story, demanding to get out of my head and onto the page. The story wrote itself.

Tune in. Write on. You may find yourself writing stories that "just write themselves."

Chapter Eleven:
We Dance

At some point while reading this book, some readers may see my take on the writing process as too simplistic, too rigid. "First you do this," I say, "then you do that, then this other thing." A linear progression. Step-by-step rote.

There is some truth to that perception. In the practice section of this book, I describe the writing process as I do because I believe you need to know what the parts are before you try to make them work together. It's like taking a rifle apart and naming the parts and putting it back together before you go to the battlefield. It's like learning the names of teeth before you practice dentistry.

It may feel, though, as if I'm naming teeth, and parts of the mouth, before I discuss how to kiss or chew gum. Who cares? It would be wrong to leave out the part where you learn not to aim your rifle at your foot, or where to put that gum when you kiss. The Big Picture.

Writing, and all art, is created holistically, another reason we're looking at *both* theory and practice here. Each phase of artistic endeavor involves the whole brain — both hemispheres — in a subtle, intensive, intricate cosmic dance. One mental aspect may lead for a nanosecond, but the other is always there, ready to lead the next turn or dip.

Both are on the dance floor together, always.

The writing process can be seen as a four-part dance where the lead shifts by degrees between brain hemispheres. This is how it's done: First, you get an idea; next, you translate that idea into a story; then you edit the story; and finally, you market the result. Your brain shifts gears progressively in each step.

1. *You get an idea.* This stage is *right-brain exclusive*, where little if any left-brain activity is involved.

2. *You transcribe the idea into a story — you write.* This stage is *right-brain dominant*. It is under right-brain control. The left brain is allowed to play, to form letters, make sentences and paragraphs and so on, but is under control of the right-brain creator and shuts up on command per the Hemisphere Accords.

3. *You edit the story you've written.* The third stage is *left-brain dominant.* Here, the left-brain is in control, handling spelling, grammar, structure, organization, and other left-brainy matters. But, if it encounters a need for a major revision, like a need to add or delete a character, or combine two characters, or a need for a new ending or opening scene, or a different setting, or a new chapter, or something like that, it can bring in the right brain. The right brain may only participate in this phase when and as directed to do so. Otherwise, it shuts up.

Many writers have developed rituals that make the editing process, in a sense, just as creative as the idea development and the writing phase. In fact, some writers say they come up with *new ideas* to put into their story during this phase. You'll have similar experiences as you write — practice — more and more.

4. *You market the story you've edited.* The final stage is *left-brain exclusive.* There is little or no place for right-brain artiness in the marketplace.

To summarize: Right-brain exclusive in the first stage shifts to right-brain dominant in the second phase, to left-brain dominant in the third, and then to left-brain exclusive in the final phase. All artists of all disciplines take the imagined and make it concrete in distinct, gradual phases.

We dance.

The trick to dancing well is to avoid stepping on your partner's toes. You learn to dance better by learning what the steps are and then practicing them. Eventually, the steps come "automatic" and you don't notice.

It works for writers too. I've concentrated in this book on describing the steps. It's up to you to practice, but now you know it isn't all step-by-step rote.

Chapter The Last:
Advanced Idea Development

Here are three notions that emerged after I achieved a deeper understanding of the creative process discussed above.

1. *The idea cluster*.

In late 1996, I conducted an experiment. How fast, I wondered, could I finish *a lot* of stories? I tried to write two stories a week for fourteen weeks. It resembled the three-stories-in-six-days on-line dare-to-be-bad challenge, but this was a marathon, not a dash.

I wouldn't have time to drive to Provo and have dinner to generate an S-V-O antenna primer for each story with my writing group. I had to have material ready to go in advance. I did so by tuning my antenna to a *cluster* of idea-generators before starting story number one.

For example, I wrote stories based on the senses—taste, touch, sight, sound, and smell. Five stories. I started "Don't Touch" *seconds* after finishing "Soul Taster." And so on. I'd finish one story and start the next, *now*, since I had a handle on the next story five stories before. The next story was already lined up on the runway, ready to take off.

I also set stories on each of the five continents. I moved from one continent to the other in alphabetical order, adding a quick S-V-O to the pre-determined setting. I did the four seasons too.

Many stories written for this experiment required a few thousand words to be cut after writing a day or two, or three. All were started with missing ingredients. With this "clustering" process, I skipped the "incubation" period discussed above, so I expected to encounter missing story elements, and was prepared. I didn't time myself, but I'll bet a few of these stories came to my mind in ninety seconds or less.

The experiment worked. I learned A Lot about my capacity to write fast, with consistent quality, and marathonishly, among other useful lessons. Sales have been good, thank you.

I've repeated this exercise many time since, and I remain happy with the results. (And by the way, I now write 2,000 to 3,000 words a day regularly. A thousand words a day is too slow.)

To summarize, here's what goes into the process:

a) I know I can write fast,

b) I know how to generate an S-V-O fast,

c) I often know in advance an extra idea-generating ingredient — senses or setting or seasons or whatever — and

d) I know the Real Story might emerge after I start, and I am prepared for it.

Whether you want to try a similar experiment, "idea-clustering," or the idea behind it, can be a useful tool in your writer's toolbox.

Consider these as possible idea-cluster generators:

— *The I-Ching.* Ancient wisdom from the mystic East. Translate into story. No messy bowls to clean.

— *The Tarot*. Ditto, but Westernish. The cards are *supposed* to tell a story.

— *The Tao Te Ching*. More eastern wisdom. Pick random phrases and shuffle.

— *The Zodiac*. Twelve characters in search of setting and plot. And a writer.

— *Astrology*. Related. Try today's newspaper horoscope for Gemini, yesterday's for Cancer, and tomorrow's for Capricorn. Three characters in search of a zodiac.

— *The Book of Lists*. Link item five on page thirty with item seven on page fifty-nine, and item three from page 167. Or vice versa.

Newspapers, TV news, the yellow pages, whatever. You get it. Make your own list.

2. *The writers group brainstorm.*

Many of us belong to writer's groups, formal or informal, groups that meet in person or via the Internet. If the primary purpose of such groups is to critique each other's manuscripts, then you can see it generally as a left-brain function. In such an atmosphere, often frank, it's wisest to leave your sensitive right brain at the door.

There are times, though, when a critique group may be used as a brainstorming session, to kick-start a project, or rejuvenate a stuck one. In such a case, leave your left brain at the door and treat the session as a drive through the desert, but this time in a car filled with right brains. Use a tape recorder. Take notes.

Be sure everybody in the group is tuned in to the same station. Using a timer might help. Ditto a "what if" list. Be flexible—right-brainish—and listen for the next antenna twist.

Again, key to success is the ability to separate your brain functions, concentrate on one hemisphere and sublimate the other. Again, it takes practice, and again, Will is ingredient number one.

3. *The Third Writer*.

When artists Leo and Diane Dillon collaborate on a project, they know the result is other than — *more* than — what either might have done alone. They talk of "the Third Artist," a creative entity that cannot exist without the energy given to a project by either one alone. The Third Artist is not just the two collaborators combined, but a new creative identity.

Does this work in writer collaborations? Diane Dillon says the concept is "the same as writers who talk about how these characters take over their work." Sounds right-brainish to me.

Bill Ransom co-wrote a trilogy with the late Frank Herbert. Ransom noted the "third artist effect," in saying "we found that we together became this third guy who wrote a little bit differently than either of us wrote." Herbert died while the third book was being drafted, and Ransom became acutely aware as he finished the book alone of that "third person" in the work.

The concept has not been explored well, to date. We see few double bylines, and fewer triple ones. We write alone. An ego thing? No two brains are alike. Sharing creative insight in converting idea to story requires two right brains in sync from start to finish, like Ransom and Herbert. If one brain shifts into left-brain mode *at the wrong time,* the project falls apart.

Ditto after the project is done, and it's time to peddle it. Any right-brain intrusion into this phase, from either party, could scuttle the boat.

Key to successful collaboration, then, is compatibility. Two minds thinking alike, a rarity, creates a third mind that thinks "other than"—*better than*—either alone.

We Dance.

Both parties (there can be more) must understand the left-brain right-brain process, even if only intuitively, and its further complication in collaboration.

Collaboration seems an attractive prospect when you consider it vis-à-vis the notions discussed in this book. Still, more work and thought needs to be done before anybody can advocate a New and Better Way to render idea into story—the Third Writer.

No doubt, there exist notions more sophisticated than these three. I'm still looking for them. The learning process never ends, and the brain is never idle.

If you have comments, suggestions—or a better way—I'd love to hear from you. E-mail me at *KRand27577@aol.com*. My web site: *www.sfwa.org/members/Rand/*.

Where do *you* get your ideas? Can you answer that in ninety seconds or less?

Reference List

Atchity, Kenneth. *A Writer's Time: A Guide to the Creative Process, from Vision through Revision*. New York: W.W. Norton & Company, 1986.

Bartlett, F.C. *Remembering*. Cambridge: Cambridge University Press, 1932.

Bayles, David and Ted Orland. *Art and Fear: Observations on the Perils (and Rewards) of Artmaking*. Santa Barbara: Capra Press, 1993.

Bentov, Itzhak. *Stalking the Wild Pendulum: On the Mechanics of Consciousness*. New York: E.P. Dutton, 1977

Bickham, Jack M. *Writing Novels That Sell*. New York: Simon & Schuster, Inc., 1989.

Blakeslee, Thomas R. *The Right Brain: A New Understanding of the Unconscious Mind and its Creative Powers*. New York: Berkley Books, 1983.

Bradbury, Ray. *Zen in the Art of Writing: Essays in Creativity: Expanded*. Santa Barbara: Joshua Odell Editions, Capra Press, 1994.

Brohaugh, William, Ed. *Just Open a Vein*. Cincinnati: Writer's Digest Books, 1987.

Campbell, Joseph. *The Hero With a Thousand Faces*. Princeton: Princeton University Press, 1949.

Chopra, Deepak. *The Seven Spiritual Laws of Success*. San Rafael: Amber-Allen Publishing, 1994.

Davis, Joel. *Mother Tongue: How Humans Create Language*. New York: Birch Lane Press, 1994.

Deming, Richard. *Sleep: Our Unknown Life*.
Nashville: Thomas Nelson, Inc., 1972.

Dimnet, Ernest. *The Art of Thinking*. New York:
Simon and Schuster, 1928.

Downey, Bill. *Right Brain, Write On!* Englewood
Cliffs: Prentice-Hall, Inc., 1984.

Ellison, Harlan, and Jacek Yerka. *Mind Fields: The
Art of Jacek Yerka, the Fiction of Harlan Ellison*.
Beverly Hills: Morpheus International, 1994.

Foster, David. *The Intelligent Universe*. New York:
J.P. Putnam's Sons, 1975.

Fryxell, David. *How to Write Fast (While Writing
Well)*. Cincinnati: Writer's Digest Books, 1992.

Gardner, John. *The Art of Fiction: Notes on Craft for
Young Writers*. New York: Vintage Books, 1985.

Gawain, Shakti. *Creative Visualization*. Novato: New
World Library, 1995.

Geng, Gia-Fu, and Jane English, translators. *Tao Te
Ching*. New York: Vintage Books, 1989.

Gerrold, David. *Worlds of Wonder: How to Write
Science Fiction & Fantasy*. Cincinnati: Writer's
Digest Books, 2001.

Gleick, James. *Chaos: Making a New Science*. New
York: Viking Penguin Inc., 1987.

Hannaford, Carla, PhD. *Smart Moves: Why Learning
Is Not All In Your Head*. Arlington: Great Ocean
Publishers, 1995.

Hartwell, David G. *Age of Wonder: Exploring the
World of Science Fiction*. New York: Tom
Doherty Associates, Inc. 1984 (1996).

Hirsch, Jr., E.D. *Cultural Literacy: What Every
American Needs to Know*. New York: Vintage
Books, 1988.

Hirshberg, Jerry. *The Creative Priority: Driving Innovative Business in the Real World*. New York: HarperCollins Publishers, Inc., 1998.

Hughes, James. *Altered States: Creativity Under the Influence*. New York: Watson-Guptill Publications, 1999.

Jung, Carl G. ed. *Man and His Symbols*. New York: Dell Publishing Co., Inc., 1964.

Jung, Carl G. *The Undiscovered Self*. New York: Little, Brown and Company, 1957, 1958.

Leader, Zachary. *Writer's Block*. Baltimore: The Johns Hopkins University Press, 1991.

Lehmkuhl, Dorothy and Dolores Cotter Lamping, C.S.W. *Organizing for the Creative Person*. New York: Crown Publishing, Inc., 1993.

Lutz, William. *Double-Speak*. New York: Harper & Row, Publishers, 1989.

McLuhan, Marshall, Quentin Fiore. *The Medium is the Massage*. New York: Bantam Books, Inc., 1967.

Moyers, Bill. *Healing and the Mind*. New York: Doubleday, 1993.

Nierenberg, Gerald I. *The Art of Creative Thinking*. New York: Barnes & Noble, 1982.

North, Anthony. *The Paranormal: A Guide to the Unexplained*. London: Cassell PLC, 1996.

Ornstein, Robert. *The Right Mind: Making Sense of the Hemispheres*. New York: Harcourt Brace & Company, 1997.

Pearce, Joseph Chilton. *The Crack in the Cosmic Egg*. New York: Washington Square Press, 1971.

Pressfield, Steven. *The War of Art: Winning the Inner Creative Battle*. New York: Rugged Land LLC, 2002.

Rand, Ken. *The 10% Solution: Self-editing for the Modern Writer*. Bonney Lake: Fairwood Press, 1998.

Rico, Gabriele Lusser. *Writing the Natural Way*. New York: J.P. Putnam's Sons, 1983.

Saks, Sol. *The Craft of Comedy Writing*. Cincinnati: Writer's Digest Books, 1985.

Shanor, Karen Nesbitt, Ph.D. *The Emerging Mind*. Los Angeles: Renaissance Books, 1999.

Shone, Ronald. *Creative Visualization: How to Use Imagery and Imagination for Self-Improvement*. Rochester: Destiny Books, 1988.

Smith, Frank. *to think*. New York: Teachers College Press, 1990.

Stott, Bill. *Write to the Point: And Feel Better About Your Writing*. New York: Columbia University Press, 1991.

Talbot, Michael. *The Holographic Universe*. New York: HarperCollins Publishers, 1991.

Underwood, Tim, & Chuck Miller, eds. *Feast of Fear: Conversations With Stephen King*. New York: Carroll & Graf Publications, Inc., 1989.

Wallas, G. *The Art of Thought*. London: C.A. Watts, 1945.

Young, James Webb. *A Technique for Producing Ideas*. Lincolnwood, IL: NTC Business Books, 1988.

Zinsser, William K. *Writing to Learn*. New York: Harper & Row, Publishers, 1988.

About the Author

Ken Rand resides with his wife and family in West Jordan, UT. He's written more than a hundred short stories, two hundred humor columns, a dozen novels, and countless articles and interviews. His Web site: **www.sfwa.org/members/ Rand/**. His living and working philosophy: Lighten up.

LaVergne, TN USA
16 December 2010
209062LV00001B/114/A